Oakley
The Lonely Oak Tree
First Edition

Written by Valerie Maurer

Illustrated by
Ronnette Benoit Manz

ISBN – 13: 978-1-7752825-0-1

I am dedicating the book to my
dear friend Michele Dionne from
Sarnia, Ontario.
It was Michele's inspiring words
and guidance to assist me to
complete the story for others to
enjoy.
Happy Reading.

Special thank you to Matlox
Publishing.
Barry your help and information
is so greatly appreciated.

The park was cold and windy.

The sun was setting.
Winter was soon here.

One tree stood alone with its shiny brown leaves whistling and crackling in the wind. His name was Oakley.

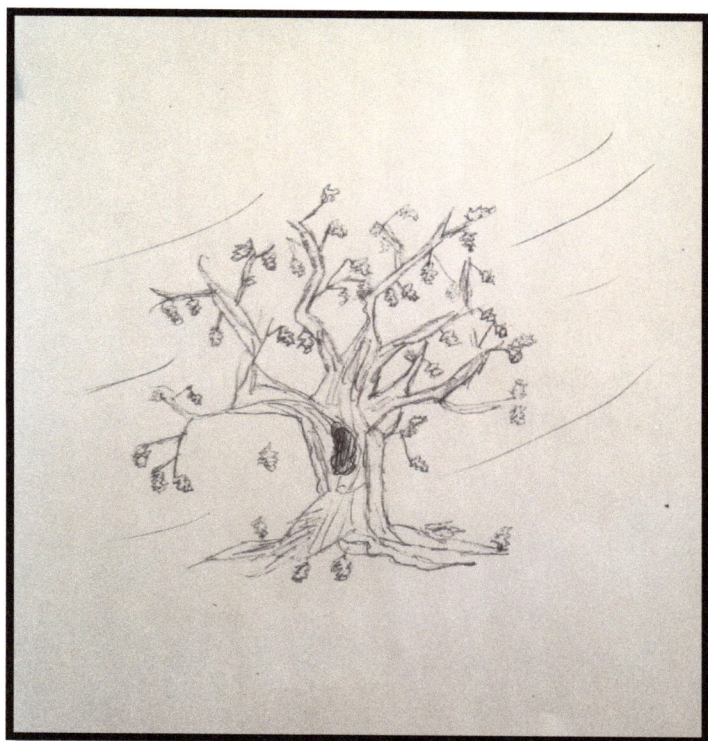

All the other trees were settling in with all their leaves laying on the ground.

The other trees were ready for winter, but that one tree, Oakley The Lonely Oak Tree.

As the sun went down it appeared the other trees were turning away from the Lonely Oak Tree.

The next day a little girl came walking thru the tree park. Dancing and singing hugging the trees. As she kicks the leaves on the ground.

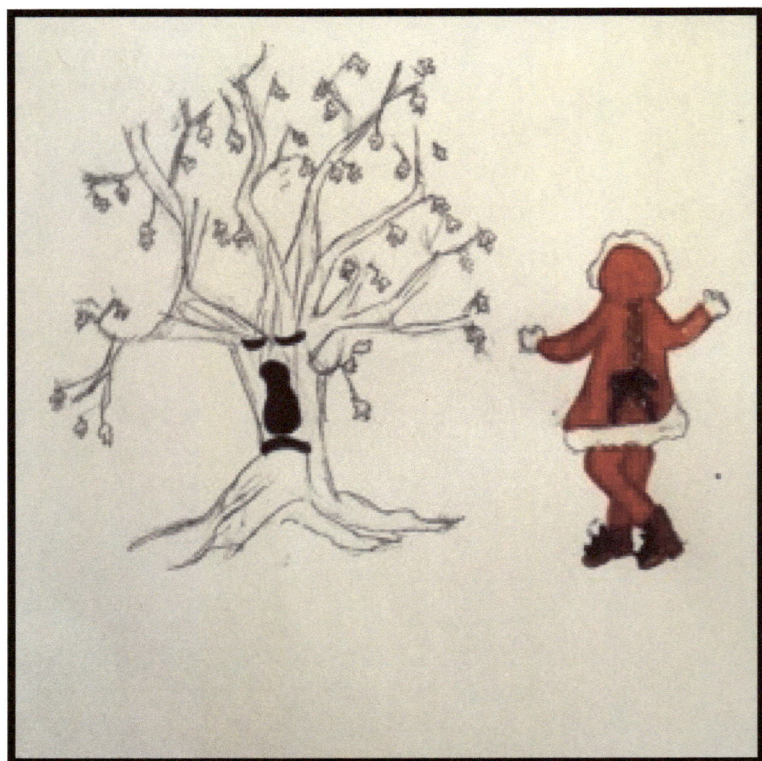

She stopped and noticed the Lonely Oak Tree with all his leaves still on his branches.

She tightly wrapped her arms around hugging Oakley the Lonely Oak Tree and said "Hurry Hurry you must lose your leaves winter is coming."

She then started to hug the other
trees asking them to be nice and
help him lose his leaves.
The Lonely Oak Tree looks
lonely and sad.

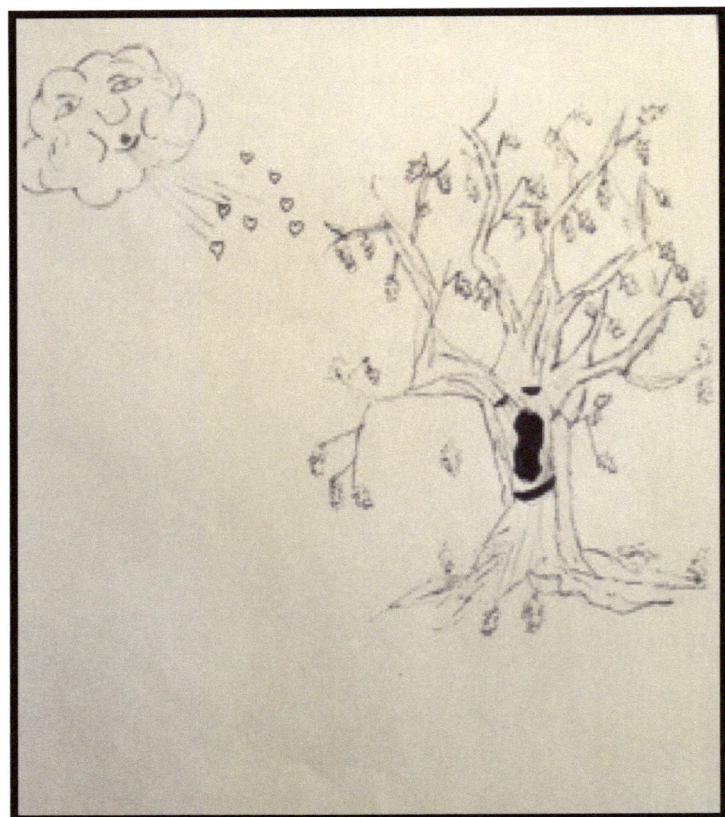

During the night as Oakley sobbed. The other trees started to sway back and forth towards the Lonely Oak Tree and blew kisses of wind.

The following day the girl
came back and notice
Oakley The Lonely Oak
had no leaves.

Oakley was smiling.

The little girl danced in the fallen leaves and thanked the other trees for helping.

Oakley, The Lonely Oak tree is no longer lonely, he is happy he lost his leaves.

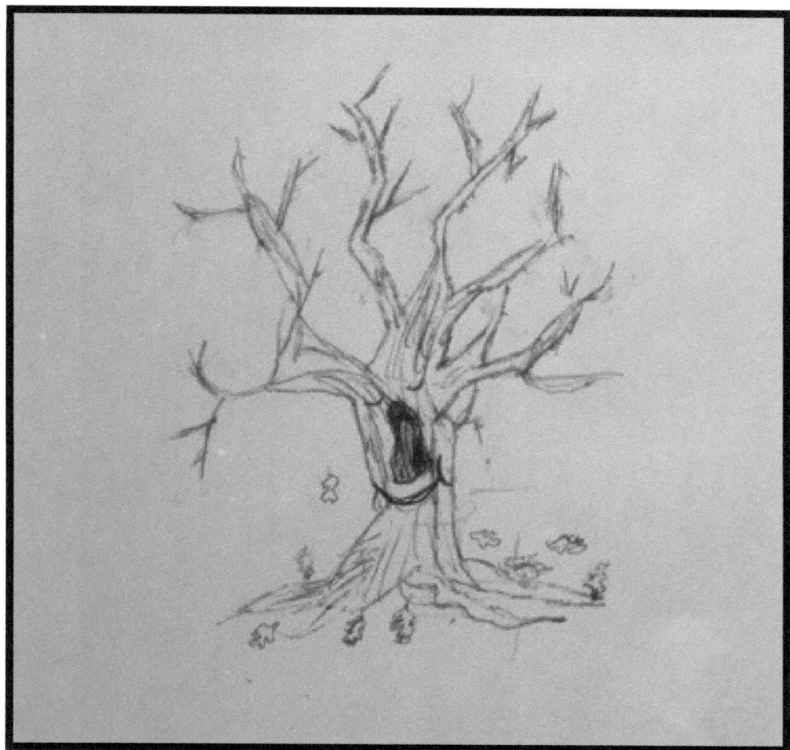

The End

Why do trees lose their leaves?

Most trees and plants lose their leaves to conserve water and to survive the cold, dry air winter conditions. In spring with warmer climate they regrow new foliage.

Draw a picture of a Oak tree.
Don't forget to put a smile on his
face, and name your tree.

Draw a picture of a leaf, as many leaves you like.
Have fun.

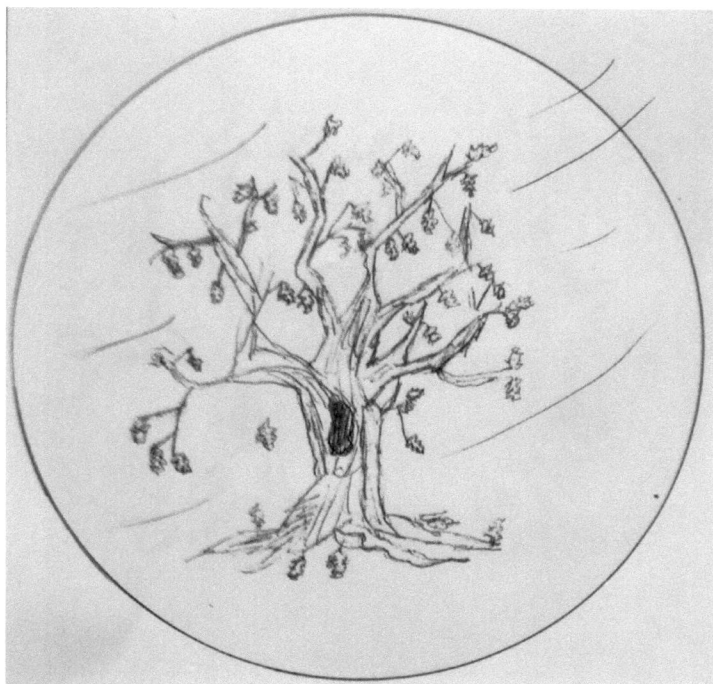

www.ingramcontent.com/pod-product-compliance
Lightning Source LLC
Chambersburg PA
CBHW041759040426
42447CB00001B/24